THE TRANSMISSION OF
AMERICAN CULTURE

THE BURTON LECTURE

1957

The Burton Lectureship

In order to stimulate interest and research in elementary education, Dr. and Mrs. William H. Burton gave to the Graduate School of Education, Harvard University, a fund for the maintenance of a lectureship under which a distinguished scholar or leader would be invited each year to discuss national problems in this field. A lectureship was accordingly established by the Graduate School of Education and named in honor of the donors. Dr. Burton, who was Director of Apprentice Teaching at Harvard for sixteen years, taught for forty-three years in the fields of elementary education and teacher education. It is hoped that these lectures will help to advance a study to which he is devoted and to which he has made distinguished contributions.

The Transmission of American Culture

George Dearborn Spindler

Associate Professor of Education and Anthropology
Stanford University

Distributed for the
GRADUATE SCHOOL OF EDUCATION
of HARVARD UNIVERSITY by
Harvard University Press
Cambridge, Massachusetts · 1962

LIBRARY OF CONGRESS CATALOG NUMBER 59–7662
PRINTED IN THE UNITED STATES OF AMERICA

PREFACE

THOUGH the range of possibilities afforded by the conjunction of cultural anthropology and elementary education is very broad, I had little difficulty in selecting a topic for the third Burton lecture. Cultural transmission has been a natural focus in my thinking since my appointment in a joint relationship to the School of Education and Department of Anthropology at Stanford University.

That this problem area is not sharply defined in the literature of education and that there has been little systematic exploration of it as a cultural process, particularly in our own society, is not surprising. Educators are only human in not discovering culture until quite recently. They are immersed in it and its processes so thoroughly that perspective is difficult.

The anthropologist has some advantages. His training and field experience should help objectify any culture for him, even his own. Study of the molding of it, the defending of it, and the communication of it from generation to generation should fall within his spectrum of interests and analytic skills. Anthropologists, however, have been more concerned with the structure and patterning of culture than they have with the way it is transmitted. Since approximately 1930, it is true, a very productive minority of anthropologists have become concerned with the relationship of personality and culture, and the dynamics of culture change. But in the framework of the first interest they focussed on the development of personality as influenced by culture and have only infrequently dealt with the communication of culture by the transmitter. In the framework of culture change they focussed on the consequences of contact between societies and their cultures but have been led to few specific formulations concerning the internal processes of transmission.

The topic of this lecture, therefore, may provide a framework within which educators and anthropologists can join forces to mutual profit. Though the presentation is exploratory, the ideas contained within it sometimes overgeneralized (particularly as we speak of American culture), and the tone of it at times more normative than objective, I have attempted to present the propositions contained within it in researchable terms.

The research of many anthropologists on the dynamics of culture and on the relationship of the individual to his culture in our own, but particularly other societies, is what makes the focus of this paper possible. Much of their work anticipates formulations presented in this lecture, and some of it advances well beyond certain of its dimensions.

The same is true of my educationist colleagues. Though the concepts they have used and the words they use to denote them are quite different from those used by anthropologists, a careful reading frequently reveals that they have been thinking along parallel lines. And they have added the results of their participant-observer experience in the educative process to their formulations. Some of Dr. Burton's own work is a fine example. In rereading one of his articles, titled "Education and Social Class in the United States" (*The Harvard Educational Review*. Fall 1953.), I was struck by the fact that he anticipates some of the same problems and processes I have discussed in this lecture.

This preface cannot be concluded without a respectful and grateful word for my students in education. These mature graduate students, returning to the university for training towards an advanced degree, are a joy to teach and work with. Their thinking is tempered by experience in the very processes we are analyzing, and they are alert to faults in my thinking to which I am blind. Lastly, and most particularly, I want to express my deep gratitude to the teachers who patiently endured my observation and study of them in their classrooms. Without their help I would have little to say.

G.D.S.

THE TRANSMISSION OF
AMERICAN CULTURE

IT IS with deep pleasure that I face the task defined by the committee for the third Burton lecture. That task is to condense the meaning of my work as a scholar in the field of anthropology for the field of elementary education.

I have selected the transmission of American culture and the teacher as a cultural transmitter as the area for discussion. Within this framework, my analysis will center on the unintended, unanticipated learning consequences in transmission that are indeed culturally patterned in themselves, but that are at variance with the intended goals of transmission.

This seems to be one of the poorly illuminated areas of educational practice and conceptualization. Discrepancies between intended educational goals—intended transmissions—and what is actually transmitted are present in curriculum design, in the literature of textbooks and teaching aids, and in classroom procedure. They permeate all phases of the student-teacher relationship, the professional education of teachers, and the very subculture of education.

The treatment of processes within this focus must be highly exploratory and incomplete, for there is so much that is unknown. But the problem is important. With more knowledge of the ways in which the goals of education are frequently defeated in the very process of education, we may achieve better control over the results of education.

Conflicts in American Culture

The source of the discrepancies and conflicts between intent and outcome, between ideal and real, that the teacher transmits to children in any classroom must be the culture. As Theodore Brameld has demonstrated so well in his new book, *The Cultural Foundations of Education*,[1] the educator must look beyond the schools and the people in them, to the culture, in order to understand the problems and the aspirations of education.

The American culture is notable for the conflicts woven into the very fabric of its value system, which is the core of any culture. For example, we appear to believe in the value of thrift, but believe even more strongly in the value of keeping up good appearances that de-

[1] Theodore Brameld, *The Cultural Foundations of Education* (Harper & Brothers, N.Y., 1957).

pend upon mortgages and installment payments that strain our budgets. We believe in deferring satisfactions to the future but want the benefits of deferment now. We believe that success is to be won by hard work, but emphasize personality and social contacts as alternative techniques. We laud honesty as a virtue but acknowledge the need for pragmatic expediency in real life. We are egalitarian in ideal and in much of our practice but indulge in wide-ranging expressions of invidious prejudices. We deny sexuality but are titillated by sex in our mass media, dress, and imagery.

There are many more such internal contradictions in our valuing system, but these suffice as examples. Our culture is patterned in conflicts that in part mirror the struggle between the puritan ethic and the demands of an industrializing society of abundance.

Convinced that educators-in-training needed to know more about these kinds of conflicts in our culture so that they could come to some resolution of them in their teaching, I began in 1952 to administer some simple value-projective techniques to my education classes. The two basic techniques were open-ended sentences, such as "The individual is —— ," "All men are born —— ," "Intellectuals should —— ," and a request that the students write a brief paragraph describing their concept of the "Ideal American Boy."

Each year since then I have analyzed the responses to these techniques from the hundred or more students in the new classes, using a form of content analysis, and have integrated the data into a treatment of education in American culture for my course lectures. What started as a pedagogical technique has become also a research project of modest dimensions. Some of the results are reported in an article published in the *Harvard Educational Review*.[2] I want to summarize the salient features of these results, both to underline the concept of patterned conflict in values in our culture and to establish the framework for a step in analysis that I will need to take later.

Brief examples of the content of the responses to these techniques are necessary. In response to the item, "Intellectuals should —," forty percent of the respondents wrote "be more sociable, more practical, more down to earth"; twenty percent wrote, "keep it under cover, drop dead, shut up"; thirty percent said, "apply their intellect, study, create, think." Approximately the same results issued from a similar item on col-

---

[2] George D. Spindler, "Education in a Transforming American Culture," *Harvard Educational Review*, 25: 145-156. Summer 1955.

lege professors, though a new category emerged —that they should "not be boring." In response to the item, "The individual is —— ," sixty percent of the respondents wrote "all-important, sacred, supreme"; twenty percent wrote, "unique, independent"; ten percent wrote "a part of the group, or the community."

Analysis of the content of the Ideal American Boy paragraphs produced a definite pattern of character values. The rank order of these values from most to least frequently mentioned is as follows: He should be sociable, well-rounded, athletic (but not an athlete), healthy, popular, clean-cut, ambitious to succeed, and considerate of others. Leadership, independence, high intelligence, high academic ability rank low in comparison to these first items. The keynote of the valued character type is balance and an outward orientation. The *social* attributes are most highly valued. Individuality, creativity are not stressed. Deviation is tolerated only within narrow limits of sociability and activistic orientation. It is clear that even with respect to trends in the sample as a whole, and without regard to patterns in individual protocols, there are certain contradictions between responses to the open-ended sentences and the content of the projective paragraphs.

Through an analysis of individual protocols,

including both responses to the open-ended items
and the paragraphic projection, it became clear
that there were essentially two basic types of
value systems represented in my sample of near-
ly six hundred students. One of them I have
labeled "traditional," the other, "emergent." The
traditional pattern includes values placed upon
thrift, self-denial, delay of satisfactions to the
future (and a belief that there will be one),
strong emphasis on success and a belief that the
means to it is hard work, a belief in absolute
morals and elevation of the *individual* as an end
rather than the group. The emergent pattern includes values placed upon sociability, sensitivity
to the feelings and needs of others, a relativistic
attitude toward moral norms, a present-time
orientation that reflects uncertainty about the
future and includes a certain kind of hedonism,
and an elevation of the harmony of the group
as an end (rather than the individual) that sub-
sumes at least resignation to group conformity.

It is apparent that these two patterns of value
are internally consistent and that they are dia-
metrically opposed. The probability of their
widespread existence helps to account for many
of the public and private arguments between
individuals and groups in our society and is re-
flected in many of the current attacks on our
educational system by the public. There is evi-

dence that educational philosophy and, to a lesser extent, practice, particularly in the elementary schools, approach the emergent typology in value orientation more closely than do the statements of the attackers, who sound, in general, like traditionalists.

But what is more significant for our purposes at the moment is that the modal pattern represented in individual protocols in my sample is a mixed type. Despite the obvious disparity in the traditional and emergent values, many people in training to become teachers, and many who have taught for a number of years and are back in school for advanced degrees, have encountered the conflict in values in their cultural environment and are making an adjustment to it, sometimes coherently, sometimes in confusion and anxiety.

I am going to make more of this later. For the moment I want to let the matter rest as a further and more specific example of the meaning of conflict in the patterning of American culture. It is usually at this point that I have to defend myself from my students, who point out that the sample is biased, that I am over-generalizing. My defense is that while, indeed, college students from the west coast may be somewhat different from college students from Harvard, and that college students are different from people who do not attend college, there is reason to think that the tendencies and patterns revealed by the procedure and this sample are present also in the distribution of values in the wider public, even though the distribution itself may vary from place to place and between different status groups. But my basic defense is that these patterns make sense with respect to institutional and personal conflicts in our society and are consistent with the interpretations of anthropologists and others, who have more intuitively described the American value system.

The Transmission of Conflicts in American Culture

It should be apparent by now that when I speak of transmitting conflicts and discrepancies in our classrooms I am not taking the overly simple stance of blaming the teacher. If the teacher is a cultural transmitter, and if teachers have experienced and, in some degree, internalized the conflicts in values that I have described, it is probable that they will transmit them to children. But I want equally as much to avoid the error of a stance that implies that because these conflicts and discrepancies are present in our culture they *should* be transmitted. If we accept this proposition, we accept the defeat and contradiction of many of our declared goals.

To illustrate concretely what is meant, permit me to describe certain educational situations in which discrepancies are transmitted. In doing so I will borrow from examples afforded by two of my anthropological colleagues as well as from my own reasearch. I have reinterpreted what my colleagues have written to fit the format of my analysis, and they can be held responsible only for the observations that provide the data.

The first example is provided by a study by Jules Henry, reported in an article "Attitude Organization in Elementary School Classrooms." [3] He points out that one of the most striking characteristics of American culture is the phenomenon of intragroup aggression, which finds its most pure expression in "witch hunts." This "witch's brew," he declares, consists of destructive criticism of others, docility, feelings of vulnerability, fear of internal (intragroup) hostility, confession of evil deeds, and boredom.

He describes a number of specific situations in elementary school classrooms where elements of this pattern are inadvertently transmitted by teachers. He does not find the full-blown pattern in the majority of classrooms in which he

[3] Jules Henry, "Attitude Organization in Elementary School Classrooms," *American Journal of Orthopsychiatry*, 27: 117–133, January 1957.

conducted research observations. But he found it in a few and was able to identify elements and tendencies in this direction in more.

For example, he describes one classroom situation where the teacher organized a Vigilance Club. The purpose of this club was to teach children to be better citizens. The club functioned as a means by which the "good deeds" and "bad deeds" of the children could be recorded in a booklet kept by the teacher for each child. Every child was required to report the wrongs and rights of his own conduct during the week, and the class was asked to contribute information about his behavior. Miscreants were placed in an "isolation ward" in the back of the room until their record was favorably balanced. In the recorded observations of this procedure it becomes abundantly clear that intragroup aggression, docility in conforming to external pressure of the group and to teacher authority, feelings of vulnerability and fear of detection, and the value of spying and confession were activated and encouraged and, therefore, transmitted. These must be regarded as unintended consequences of the teacher's purposeful action, since the intended purpose was to encourage good citizenship. These unintended consequences did not appear out of a vacuum. The pattern was already available in the culture, was present in varying degrees of latency in the children, but was activated in the behavioral setting created by the teacher.

This is admittedly an extreme example, and is cited as almost a caricature of what normally happens in many classrooms. Let me extract another less extreme illustration from those provided by his work. In one fifth grade classroom the period was devoted to short reports and stories by the children. The class was requested by the teacher to criticize each report. Children responded by pointing out that the sentences were too short, there was too much detail, there was too little expression, and so on. No positive criticisms emerged, nor did the teacher seek out any. Probably many teachers would do so, since they would realize that criticism by one's peers, particularly at that age level, is more likely to be destructive than constructive. But the net effect of this procedure was to support children in their tendency to be carpingly critical of their fellows and, therefore, to contribute to the development of patterns of intragroup aggression that were already internalized in some degree by the children from their culture. The experience was organized by the teacher, however, for the purpose of increasing skill in writing and reporting, and also, I infer, to contribute to learning to "take criticism"—one of the frequently cited criteria for good adjustment. The contradiction of ends and means is apparent.

I would like to provide another documentation of the processes involved in transmitting cultural discrepancies in educational situations. This example is applicable to both elementary and secondary education. Dorothy Lee has attempted to answer this question: "What covert attitudes and concepts are communicated through the home economics program in public schools?" Her analysis may be found in the book, *Education and Anthropology*.[4] She makes it explicit that the study is concerned with that which is communicated implicitly, unintentionally, and contrary to the intention of the program. Her paper has been particularly influential in the development of my own thinking on the matter.

Professor Lee used fifteen state and city manuals for teachers of home economics, representing different regions, and one textbook in common use, as sources of data. Admittedly, teachers deviate from manuals in actual instruction. This study therefore provides illustration of the fact that cultural discrepancies are found

[4] Dorothy Lee, "Discrepancies in the Teaching of American Culture," in *Education and Anthropology*, ed. George D. Spindler (Stanford University Press, 1955).

in the design of classroom procedures and not only in their implementation.

These programs, it is stated in the manuals, are designed to help the student develop a healthy personality through participation in human relations in the home, and to help students mature into adults who will establish democratic, happy, cooperative homes, as well as to pass on the skills necessary for home-making.

She cites a number of instances where the design of the manuals can be interpreted as introducing contradictions to this purpose. For example, in one manual, presumably not atypical, the lesson on family relationships states other objectives: to realize the purpose of restrictions, to realize one's contributions to family conflict, and to help the student to learn ways of reducing conflict. The student is to relate herself to a family life that is full of conflict and restriction. "Why do parents always say 'no'?" "What can a boy or girl do about a 'pesky' sister or brother?"—these are some of the questions posed for the student.

Other examples drawn from those she provides include the contradiction between the declared goal of learning to share meaningful experiences in the home and an implementation of this goal in curriculum design that provides great detail on selecting recipes, nutritional needs, finishing seams and doing laundry, but nothing on who shares these activities or who is being helped. Another dualism is conveyed by the declared emphasis on creative enjoyment of the home and of family living but an implementation in design that characterizes housekeeping as work that needs to be done efficiently so that one can have more leisure time away from it all. Only escape has value. Ordinary home life seems to provide little emotional nourishment. And, lastly, another declared goal is to develop mature personalities (that development, presumably, requires some sustenance for the inner self), but it is solely the external characteristics of good grooming, pleasant manners, being popular and making friends, being efficient about one's expenditure of time that are stressed.

Since I had the privilege of acting as chairman for the seminar-conference of educators and anthropologists where Professor Lee's paper was presented and discussed, I am not unfamiliar with the resentful objections that this kind of analysis arouses. I think it is only fair to point out that Dorothy Lee herself felt that her interpretation might have been biased by certain personal values that she holds because she was a Greek before she was an American. Apparently a happy home life, sharing family activities, enjoying the ordinary routine of family living, and developing a self-actualized personality are valued in Greek culture. But I have always thought they were valued in American culture as well. What is important for our purposes here is that the design of the manuals for home-making includes these values as goals but also includes designs for implementation that are in varying degrees of contradiction to them. In one sense this design is an accurate projection of American culture. This makes it all the more important that the contradictions be treated with awareness and objectivity and, perhaps in some instances, reduced or eliminated.

For my last example of direct transmission of obvious but culturally patterned contradictions, I would like to cite briefly from one of my own case studies of teachers and their classrooms. Later on I will describe a more complex situation.

The cultural transmitter in this case was a highly respected teacher in a large elementary school, who had certain duties as a counselor. He originated from a respectable immigrant family and had improved his social status during his lifetime by becoming a schoolteacher. The particular situation from which I have extracted certain verbatim records to follow was one of the "rites of passage" that occur now and then throughout the educational life cycle of children. The students in the eighth grade were being prepared for the choice of programs in high school and were making out proposed study lists under his guidance. The class group consisted of thirty-five children, twenty-four of whom were Mexican–Americans. The range of scores on the California Mental Maturity test was eighty to one hundred and twenty, with a median of 102. There was a broadly corresponding variety of reading and academic achievement represented in the group. I will present a few items from the verbal interaction of the teacher-counselor and the students.

T: "You must be a good citizen, or they won't accept you. Now, what do you need to get into Orthodox State College? *(Children raise hands, repeat answers previously learned.)* What do you need to get into Junior College?" *(Students respond likewise.)*

T: "In arranging your programs for next year, there are certain things that everyone must take, so we'll just put them down. You will all take P. E., English, and Social Studies. *(Teacher writes these down on the board opposite numbers 1, 2, and 3.)* Now you have to decide whether you want to take Algebra or not. You have to take math all the way through high school if you want to be an engineer. Now, if you've gotten B's and C's all the way through eighth grade, what are your chances of doing well in ninth grade Algebra? *(Students murmur various things).* That's right! Not so good! So what can you do?"

S: "Try to raise your grade."

T: "Yes."

S: "Work harder."

T: "That's one thing. But what else? . . . Do like I did when I wanted to be a singer but found I couldn't sing. What did I do? Yes . . . that's right; I changed my plans. . . . With respect to language, how many here speak Spanish? *(Six of the Mexican–Americans raised their hands, but all speak some Spanish.)* It will help you if you do. But you have to realize that there is some work to do—homework! It is good to take Spanish if you want to go on to college and need a language. But you can't take Spanish and General Business. They come at the same period. Now, one of the things you have to do is to be neat and orderly. If you aren't good at that it might be hard for you until you learn to do it better."

T: "Now here we have Mechanical Drawing. This is exclusively a boy's class. I don't know why some girls couldn't take it if they wanted to. But only boys take it. Now Home-making is for girls, so you can take that."

T: "Now when you come to see me, if I tell you

to take General Business instead of Spanish, it should be understood that you don't have to take it. You can do as you wish. But it means that I think you will do better in General Business." *(Several more subject choices are covered).*

T: "And here is typing. It looks interesting when you pass the typing room, doesn't it? But do you know there aren't any letters on those keyboards? You have to watch a chart at the front of the room, and if you look at the keyboard, you fail!"

Of course a great deal more went on during this hour of counseling. I have purposefully selected those verbal items that constitute the most clear indications of bias in cultural transmission. And this is always unfair to the cultural transmitter. But I believe the extracted items accurately reveal persistent trends in his counseling of the mixed Mexican–American and Anglo-groups in the eighth grade.

After this particular class session, the teacher-counselor said, "This is a passive group. There is no spark in there. The better groups get quite excited about this. Of course, most of the better groups are college-preparatory and perhaps only three or four of these students will go to college." Previous to the session, in his statement of educational philosophy, he had commented,

"I believe that our job is to make the most of
the potential of each child. Of course there is
a wide range of ability among our students.
A good many of them will never go on to college. And we have to do the best we can to help
them on to a satisfactory adjustment."

I propose that he was defeating his own aims
in the way he handled this crucial rite of passage, this point of compression in the relation of
the child and his culture where choices made
affect future development decisively. He opened the gates to valued channels of development
and then shut them in the children's faces. And
he did not open the gates to any alternative
channels. What he transmitted, it seems to me,
was that the only worthwhile goal was to go
to college so that one could become an engineer
or something equivalent, that if the child did
not have the necessary qualifications there was
no other dignified and worthy choice, and that
most of the members of this class group did not
have the necessary qualifications.

I would be less concerned if I thought this
person were a small, mean individual with
explicit prejudices, and if I thought he were
not concerned with making the most of the
potential of each child. But he is not small and
mean. He is a generous, well-intended person,
and believes in democratic opportunity. In his

counseling he projects his own struggle to improve his status, mirrors the discrepancy in our
culture between ideal and real in the definition
of opportunity, and inadvertently defeats his
own professed aims.

The Acculturation of the School Teacher

What I hope has been established so far is that
our culture is one in which conflicts in values,
and between goals and the means to them, are
present and patterned. And that teachers, as
cultural transmitters, convey these patterned
conflicts to children in their classrooms, with the
consequence that many professed goals are defeated, or at least obscured. I hope that it is also
clear that I have not been castigating teachers.
They are the agents of their culture.

A further step must be taken if we are to see
the full meaning and scope of the problem.
Teachers are a special group. They are not
selected at random as official culture transmitters; they are trained and accredited to that
status and role. They must take courses in educational psychology, the social foundations of
education, curriculum design, philosophy and
history of education, the methods of education,
and must do supervised practice teaching. In
short, they must attend teacher-training institu-

tions and graduate with the stamp of approval
from the established professional cadre. But professional educational instruction and training
consist not alone of courses and training in
techniques. Every institution with a history and
internal organization, and a specialized personnel, has a culture—or more properly—a subculture. Certain values, symbols, beliefs, and
certain basic premises are patterned into the
structure and process of the institution. The institutions of professional education—the teacher-
training schools and the literature of education
—are no exception.

What I am going to try to say now may be
misunderstood. I am going to state some
generalizations about the subculture of education. Some of my educational colleagues will
disagree, but objectively. Others will disagree,
and be offended. Some will agree and approve.
Others will agree but be unhappy about doing
so.

I must refer back to the traditional and emergent value patterns revealed in the responses of
education students to the values projection
techniques. You will remember that the traditional pattern included emphasis on thrift, self-
denial, faith in the future, a strong emphasis on
success and a belief that hard work was the
means to it, absolute moral norms, and a strong

value placed upon the individual as an end. The emergent pattern included value placed upon sociability, sensitivity to the feelings of others, a relativistic attitude, a present-time orientation, and high value placed upon the group. The modal type of person with respect to these dichotomous value patterns is a mixed type that embraces values from both in varying degrees of coherence.

I believe that many of the conflicts between school boards and educational personnel, between parents and teachers, and between teachers and pupils can be seen as projections of differences in value commitments that represent various approximations to the traditional and emergent positions. But the dynamic process of greatest relevance to us at the moment is the relationship between the culture that the elementary school teacher brings to the professional teacher-training institution subculture, and the patterning of that subculture, the adaptation that the teacher-in-training makes to this patterning, and the consequences in selective culture transmission in the classroom.

This is a complex relationship with many subtle ramifications. I must dissect it with bold and clumsy slashes rather than precise incisions. It is well established that school teachers originate from a middle and lower-middle social class culture. I believe that it can also be demonstrated that the value pattern that I have termed "traditional" is found in this cultural context in its most purely puritanic form. To the extent this is so, it means that whatever selective processes are operating tend to bring many people of traditionalistic value orientation into teacher-training.

The question that the anthropologist raises is—what are the characteristics of the subculture of the teacher-training institution to which these students bring their traditionalist orientations? Analysis of a sample of some of the influential literature of curriculum design for elementary education reveals that there is present a strong values bias that fits in general terms the "emergent" pattern. The literature of child development and educational psychology reveals some of the same trends. Interpretations of the social behavior of boys and girls, intended for educational consumption, provide both implicit and explicit value judgments in the same pattern. The popularity of sociometric techniques is diagnostic of this orientation. The topical content of many of our teacher-training courses suggests it as well.

The basic premise underlying the superstructure of specific emergent values is that what is most important is the social adjustment of the child. His place in the group, the responses of his peers to him, his ability to get along well, to work and play with others are penultimate concerns. I personally do not regard this as all bad. The emphasis on social adjustment is the educator's attempt to meet the demands of a new kind of society, where this kind of adjustment is of vital importance. When balanced by a concern for individual differences, support for the deviating child, for intellectual development and the acquiring of cognitive skills, and when it does not become a form of "groupism," this emphasis on social adjustment is a necessary compensation for what I regard as many of the harshly competitive, egocentric patterns of our culture.

But the point is that however understandable and useful the emphasis may be, this pattern of values incorporated in the ethos of professional education may be at variance with what the new teacher in training brings into the situation. The neophyte in training must reorient his value system wherever the conflict in values is encountered.

This places many new teachers in training in a situation similar to that of acculturating populations all over the world. These populations are attempting to rechannel their emotional and intellectual commitments as they adapt to conflicts between their indigenous culture and the new culture diffused to them or appropriated by them. Anthropological studies of such populations provide the models for characterizations of adaptive consequences for teachers that I wish to make now, but these models are rebuilt in terms of empirical case studies of teachers in classrooms.

When acculturating teachers in training or people in any other acculturating group adapt to sharply disjunctive value systems, essentially four adaptive responses may occur. The individual meets the new value system and feels threatened because it challenges his established, familiar, and comfortable values. He does not, of course, necessarily interpret the experience in these terms. He is more likely to see it as a personal conflict, which heightens the threat. After some exploration in the new dimensions of feeling and belief offered to him by the opposing system, his feeling of threat overcomes him and he seeks refuge in the comforting shelter of his established values. But something has changed. He has been driven back to his "native state" by threat. Therefore he overcompensates, and rigidifies the original system in what may be psychologically termed a reaction formation, or culturally termed a "nativistic reaffirmation." I would call him a "reaffirmative traditionalist" in the framework of this analysis. The teacher of this type will tend to be rigid in his uncompromising projection of traditional values in his classroom behavior.

An alternative adaptive response is represented by the person who encounters the new value system which is sharply disjunctive with his own, likewise feels threatened by the conflict in personal terms, but adapts by overcompensating in the direction of the new system. Perhaps he is more threatened by the possibility of being left behind or out of step than he is by the requirement to change. He uncritically appropriates the new values in their entirety and frequently becomes a strident proselytizer for them. This kind of teacher I term a "compensatory emergentist." His channels of communication with children, and his criteria for their behavior, become narrowed to individual-in-harmony-with-the-group. "Groupism" reigns in his classroom. Individualistic differences and deviations become smothered by group conformity.

The third alternative adaptive response is exhibited by the person who encounters the conflict of value systems and superficially internalizes segments of both but does not rework them into any coherent synthesis. He is a mixed type but quite different from a type that I shall describe shortly. He is usually not particularly thoughtful about the conflicts he encounters and leaves them unresolved, but still a part of his acquired culture. This person as a teacher is likely to vacillate between different modes of group leadership and different modes of interaction with individual children. Obvious discontinuities in his classroom management cause trouble for both him and his students. I term his type, the "vacillator."

The fourth alternative is a happier one than either of the others. This person comes into the acculturative situation with a capacity for adjustment to differences in values and conflicts between them. Usually he is thoughtful and has the ability to combine useful features from more than one system of belief on a rational basis. He does not need to overcompensate as a defense against conflict because he is not threatened by it. He is a mixed type but does not internalize the mixture segmentally. He recombines the aspects from both systems into a creatively coherent synthesis. I have labeled this an "adjusted" type.

As a matter of fact I believe increasing numbers of students in our senior and graduate education classes are of this latter type. They exhibit workable combinations of what seem to be the best of both the emergent and traditional values. For instance, they accept the need of the individual to be a member of the group but believe that the individual must be self-possessed and self-actualized in order to be a useful participant in any group. They believe that hard work is necessary for success but that there is no point in being unpleasant about it. Whether they represent a shift in the kind of training they receive in the school of education, or whether they represent a change in the culture of generations, or both, I do not know. In any event, I am happy to see them and hope their numbers increase, for I am convinced that large numbers of teachers, at least new ones, are reaffirmative traditionalists, compensatory emergentists, or vacillators.

I make a value judgment here because it seems clear to me that teachers falling into the first two adaptive categories tend to exhibit highly selective biases as culture transmitters. They transmit in narrow channels with few alternatives, due to their reactive rigidity. Without intending to do so, they open some doors to self-cultivating developments for some children but lock them for many others. And the vacillator, though he is not rigid and transmits along many channels, issues only weak signals and produces little but static as a result.

A Case Study Illustration

To illustrate further what I mean, I would like to describe one case study that is representative of others I have made of elementary school teachers and their classrooms. There are case studies in my files that represent each of the four adaptive responses that I have described. I will present the salient features of only one case, and I classify this one as a reaffirmative traditionalist. The choice is based on the opinion that this type is more frequently encountered in other parts of the country than it is in California (where my observations have been made), and the analysis should have wide applicability.

This fifth-grade teacher is a young man of twenty-five. He originates from a clearly traditionalistic middle class family. His father is an executive of middle rank in a wholesale business organization who belonged to the usual service and fraternal organizations. His mother is college-educated and active in the League of Women Voters. His father is not college-educated and achieved his position by hard work and brains. Both parents like to play bridge, belong to the country club and own a summer cottage where the subject spent many happy leisure hours as a boy. Twice during the subject's lifetime the family moved to more expensive homes in better neighborhoods.

The subject likes to play golf, drinks socially but moderately, attends the Methodist church, and reads the local newspaper, *Reader's Digest*, and the *Saturday Evening Post*. He aspires to be a school administrator and regards his teaching experience as preparation for that role. He is a pleasant, good-looking young man who appears somewhat constrained but not visibly anxious. He is well liked by his colleagues and is rated as one of the outstanding young teachers in the school system.

His professed aims in teaching, beyond the management of instruction so that his students acquire the requisite knowledge, are to bring out creativity to the maximum ability of each child, help children to express themselves clearly and help children to learn how to get along with each other. He states that he tries to give every student in his class a chance to participate. He prides himself particularly on being fair and just with all the children. He says explicitly that every student gets a "fair break" in his classroom. He feels that he is very concerned about the problems of his students and always tries to understand them. His statements about his aims and his relations with his students are consistent with what his principal, his supervisor, and the members of the central staff of the school system say about him.

He told me that many of his teacher-training courses were "a waste of time." In probing this blanket indictment of professional educational preparation as he experienced it I discovered that he was dismayed and upset by certain points of view that he perceived as consistently appearing in his course work. He felt that his preceptors were trying "to give the school to the children," that they were more concerned with how children adjusted than what they learned, and that his instructors stressed cooperation, or at least group harmony, at the expense of competition. All of this he lumps together under the label "progressive education," which he rejects with feeling, but which he is content to leave as an unanalyzed abstraction. I hasten to add that I do not think his instructors in the professional education courses he took want to give the school to the children, or were unconcerned with learning. But he perceived them that way, and the reason I think he did was because he was encountering for the first time, under conditions of pressure, the emergent-oriented values system. His perception may be skewed because he was threatened.

He fits the criteria for the reaffirmative-traditionalist teacher type. He originated from a family culture where the traditional values I have described apparently existed in virtually pure form. He encountered the emergent-oriented values of the professional teacher-training subculture. He sensed the conflict, felt the threat, rejected the threatening alternatives, and sought refuge in the shelter of his original values. If he seems to fit too well, I can only say that the typology was constructed with empirical cases of this type as part of the data.

My further presentation of data on this teacher and his classroom will include a few items selected from a considerable mass of information. We worked together for many months, and his file is extensive. But these few items will establish the pattern that permeated many of the interrelationships between him and his students.

One of our standard practices in case studies is to ask the teacher to fill out a form titled "Information Concerning the Student." It includes items on academic and social adjustment in the child's previous school, his home situation, approximate I.Q. test performance, special interests, hobbies, health history, his ambitions and plans for the future. The teacher is requested to fill out this form for each student without recourse to written records. He is scored on the number of items of information. A perfect score, indicating highest knowledge, would be ten.

This teacher averaged 3.2 for the forms filled out on all of his thirty-three students, which is lower, on the average, than the score attained by other teachers in our sample. The mean of his knowledge concerning children in his group originating from families of highest socio-economic status was 4.9. His mean score for those of lowest status was 2.8. It is immediately apparent that some bias is operating that tends to contradict his professed aims.

He was asked to list the names of those students in his class that he considered to be the best adjusted—emotionally and socially. Of the seven children he listed as best adjusted only one child was included who originated from a family of less than middle-class status, and this child exhibited strong status-achievement drives. He was also asked to list the names of those students whom he considered least well adjusted. Of these seven children, only one came from a middle-class setting. The other six were from families of lower-class status. It is possible, of course, that he was correct in his appraisal, even from a psychiatric point of view. Other evidence concerning the behavior of these children indicates that he was not accurate in a number of instances. For our purposes at the moment what is significant is that the same bias in perception is revealed in this bit of data as was exhibited in his knowledge about students.

He was asked to list the 25 percent of his class group with whom he thought he had the most effective relationship. He listed eight children, and of these eight, five were from families of middle-class social status. He was also asked to list the 25 percent of his group with whom he felt he had the least effective relationship. All but one of these children were from families of lower-class status. Other evidence indicates that in this instance he appraised the situation more or less accurately. The pattern of selective perception, of differential bias in his interrelationships with children in his class group is, however, strengthened.

He was requested to name those children who were the most popular with or most accepted by their classmates. He listed eight, only one of whom represented a lower-class position. In only three instances did he name the same children that the students themselves did, according to sociometric information collected from the class. He was also asked to name those children, to whom nobody in the class paid much attention. He listed six children, two of whom were middle-class in origin. The other four were from families of lower-class status. In four instances his perceptions matched those of the classroom group, but there were ten comparatively isolated

children in that group, according to the sociometric data collected from the class. Of these
ten, five were children originating from middle-
class backgrounds, four of whom he missed in
his appraisal. Again, there is a clear pattern of
selective bias in his perception of the children
in his classroom. It is difficult for him to imple-
ment his professed aims in the context of this
pattern.

A few excerpts from anecdotal and verbatim
records will strengthen the interpretation. One
boy, who was quite isolated sociometrically in
the interactive patterns among the boys in the
class and who chose only girls in his own sociometric responses, was described by the teacher
as a "real go-getter, one of the most magnetic
personalities of any young child I have ever
known. He has a very warm personality—truth-
ful, sincere, with a good sense of humor. Tom
gets along well with anyone, anywhere." This
boy sometimes brought small bottles of hair
tonic, shoe polish, simple toys and gadgets to
class in a small suitcase and tried to sell them to
the other children. One day when I was observ-
ing, he was allowed to "make his pitch" before
the class. He was, indeed, a motivated, magnetic,
salesman, and probably will go far. The teacher
apparently perceived only this attribute—one
that is congruent with some of his own achieve-

ment drives and their precedents in his family models. There is much else about this child that he needed to know in order to guide his development effectively.

In another instance of the same type the teacher described one girl as having a "horrible personality . . . egoistic, insincere, false. She never has a nice word to say about anyone but herself. I don't particularly care for Charlotte." She was the friendship choice of the "star-of-attraction"—the girl most frequently chosen as a friend by the other girls in their sociometric responses. She was observed to interact effectively with most of the other girls. She had a high rating in status-reputation data collected from one class. She came from a broken home in a lower-class setting.

In his response to oral reports by the children about what they were reading in their spare time, his gestures, facial expression, bodily postures, comments and silences were all patterned in the framework of the same selective bias. He communicated approval of most of what the children of middle-class origins said, and of what they were reading. He communicated lack of interest, or suppressed distaste for what the children of lower-class origins said, how they said it, and of what they were reading.

I have almost too much data on this teacher

and his classroom, and have had to struggle against the inclination to continue with examples that all substantiate the same pattern of bias and selective perception in his relationships with his students. He interacted effectively with only a minority segment of his classroom group—that segment which matched his own aspirations and values, derived from his own cultural setting. He opened doors for this selected group to channels of development they were already heading toward, and he sped them on their way. But for the larger number of his students, those who did not match his values and aspirations, he closed doors and left them waiting in the foyer of our culture.

Analysis of all of the data collected about this teacher and his operations in the classroom has led me to the conclusion that his consistent selectivity of interaction was in part due to his own cultural background. But this pattern was accentuated by his reactive adjustment to the conflict between the culture he brought with him when he entered professional training to become a teacher and the special subculture he encountered there.

His exercise of the role of cultural transmitter was in contradiction to his own professed aims, and even to his own beliefs about what he actually did in the classroom. He was not giving all children an opportunity to participate; he did not understand their problems; he was not being fair and just to all his students; they were not all getting a "fair break." All these aims and beliefs were contradicted by his highly selective positive interaction with a small segment of his class. He was wearing cultural blinders that limited his perceptions to a single channel. His transmitting apparatus was sending out positive signals only to that segment responding within the frequency of that single channel.

A Cross-cultural Perspective

Now I would like to apply a cross-cultural perspective to this case and some of the inferences drawn from it. In one of my seminars we have been reviewing the available literature on the educative process in a wide variety of non-literate, so-called "primitive" societies. One of the concepts we have found particularly useful is one we have termed "cultural compression." The meaning of the term is simple. It refers to any period of time in the life cycle of the individual when he encounters a culturally patterned reduction of alternatives for behavior. During these periods, culturally normative restrictions are placed upon him. They are the points in his development as a creature of culture when the norms of his group and society bear in upon him with the greatest intensity. I will apply this concept to the educational process in cultures other than our own, and then return to a brief reconsideration of the educative process in our society and the case of our teacher in this broadened perspective.

Cultural compressions may be detected in the life cycle in any society at a number of developmental stages. Toilet training and weaning are forms of cultural compression. So is induction to work. Culturally patterned preparations for assumption of adult roles are particularly critical points in the compressive sequence. In our examination of the literature available on forty non-literate societies we have isolated a number of types of cultural compression sequence. We find that we can even draw graphs of them. Imagine two horizontal lines of equal length, one above the other. Place the newborn infant at one end between the lines and start him through his developmental stages. Contract the lines in such a way as to portray the points in his progressive experience where cultural restrictions are placed upon him. Expand them so as to portray the points in his experience where cultural restrictions are lifted as they no longer become appropriate to his age and status. This imagery should serve to indicate the kinds of models we have constructed. I will not attempt to communicate verbally the specific nature of any types.

We find that the types differ sharply from each other in the sequence of cultural compressions during the prepubertal years. We find in all of them, however, that the channels of self and cultural development become progressively narrowed as time goes on. Eventually most alternative channels are eliminated, and only a single major one (but possibly several secondary ones) is provided for each sex. In order to insure that the cultural boundaries of this channel are internalized by the developing individual many societies introduce dramatically compressive restrictions at the time of puberty in the form of initiation ceremonies. In many societies this period is a time of very intensive training and of very severe restriction. Dramatic rituals, isolation from home and familiar surroundings and people, the use of forbidding strangers as instructors, heighten the effect of the restrictions and cultural transmissions that occur at this time. And there is only one correct major channel into which the initiate is compressed. Permit me to quote from a paper by C. W. M. Hart that has stimulated my thinking in this direction. He describes the initiation experience among the Tiwi of North Australia. "So far his life has been easy; now it is hard. . . The boy of twelve

or thirteen, used to noisy, boisterous irrespon-
sible play, is expected and required to sit still
for hours and days at a time, saying nothing
whatever but concentrating upon and endeavor-
ing to understand long intricate instructions and
"lectures" given him by his hostile and forbidding preceptors. Life has suddenly become
real and earnest and the initiate is required
literally to 'put away the things of a child,' even
the demeanor. The number of tabus and unnatural behaviors enjoined upon the initiate is
endless. He mustn't speak unless he is spoken to;
he must eat only certain foods and often only
in certain ways; at certain fixed times and in
certain fixed positions. All contact with females,
even speech with them, is rigidly forbidden, and
this includes mother and sisters. He cannot even
scratch his head with his own hand, but must
do it with a special stick, and so on, through a
long catalogue of special, unnatural, but oblig-
atory behaviors covering practically every
daily activity and every hour of the day and
night." [5] Professor Hart continues in his de-
scription, but I believe that this will communicate what I mean by the notion of compression
to a single channel.

This technique of cultural transmission ap-

[5] C. W. M. Hart, "Contrasts Between Prepubertal and
Postpubertal Education," in *Education and Anthropology*,
ed. Spindler, p. 136.

parently works very well in many small, non-literate societies. They are comparatively homogeneous in value systems, there being a limited range of values within which every member of the society is committed. Specialization in roles and statuses is at a minimum.

There are personality differences between members of the society, but they cluster around the cultural promontories afforded by the traditional values and prescribed roles. The society and its culture are stable, tradition-oriented, and unchanging, compared to ours. The highly compressive techniques are effective because the cultural boundaries and barriers imposed upon the growing individual are consistent with the character and limitations of the culture as a whole. Alternative channels for development are not needed as long as the equilibrium of the culture is not seriously disturbed.

But it is easy to make the mistake of assuming that because these techniques of cultural transmission work well in the comparatively simple, non-literate societies they will work for us also. Our society is extraordinarily complex with respect to the specializations required of individuals and the multiple roles and statuses provided for these specializations. And although our value system has some coherence, the alternatives are impressive, and the conflicts within it even more so. A single-channel type of cultural transmission is dysfunctional in our society. It is dysfunctional because we need variety of outlook, skills, and personality types in order to maintain our internal complexity. And if we are to adapt successfully to the rapidly changing conditions of existence forecast by the opening events of the atomic age and the first tentative steps towards the exploration of outer space and other worlds, we must provide, in our cultural transmission, for innovative channels of self and cultural development.

I think my point is clear. This teacher not only defeated some of his own educational aims in his classroom management, but he transmitted within only a single channel. He did not intend to do so, to be sure. This is precisely why his case is of interest to us. None of the illustrations of cultural transmission that I have described were examples of wilful, intentional, misconstruing of the teacher's role. It is because cultural processes of this sort are difficult to perceive, particularly when one is caught up in them, that I selected this topic for discussion.

Cultural Therapy

So that we do not lose focus, I will summarize briefly the major points that I have tried to communicate. I will then go on to a consideration of steps we might take towards a solution, and conclude with a statement of some unresolved dilemmas.

I started with an analysis of conflicts in the patterning of American culture, and attempted to illustrate, through examples borrowed from the writings of Jules Henry and Dorothy Lee, and extracted from my own case records, how these conflicts were transmitted in our schools, with emphasis on the elementary years. I also tried to show how in the act of transmission, the professed aims of teachers were sometimes defeated and contradicted. I then moved on to an analysis of the conflict between the cultural values many teachers bring with them into professional training and those subsumed in the culture of the teacher-training institutions, and of the adaptive consequences of this conflict. The case study of the fifth-grade teacher was used to demonstrate the selective and goal-defeating process of cultural transmission that I believe to be characteristic of one of the adaptive types. I then shifted the emphasis from the transmission of culture conflicts to the problem of single-channel transmission, and tried to demonstrate that this process was not only contradictory to the teacher's professed aims, but also dysfunctional in our complex, changing society. Throughout, I have maintained that as an agent of culture the teacher is not to be personally blamed for the consequences described.

We cannot let the matter rest there. It is true, I believe, that the teacher is activating a precedent cultural condition in the process of transmission. It is also true that because this is so, changes are difficult to bring about, since the problem is of extraordinary scope. The total structure of our society and the patterning of our culture is involved. But because this is a problem in cultural process, I am going to propose a first step in solution that I will term "cultural therapy." This concept is closely allied to one communicated to me by Lawrence K. Frank, that he labels "cognitive therapy." [6]

I did not describe my role in the teacher case studies that I used for illustrative purposes. It has a direct bearing upon the notion of "cultural therapy." I was a member of a team that had a dual purpose—to collect case study data on the basic processes of education and to work in a close relationship with our teacher cases to improve their professional competence. We made no effort to select "problem" cases, and neither of these I have cited materials from were defined as such. We merely operated on the assumption that all teachers were interested in improving

[6] In private conversation.

their professional competence. Each member of the team took responsibility for certain cases, but we consulted with each other throughout both the research and consultative phases of the studies.

In the consultative phase of all cases we fed back to the teacher the data we had collected in the research phase. The completeness, timing, sequence, and interpretation of this "feedback" differed for each case. Some teachers can tolerate their objective image more easily than others. The fifth-grade teacher I described was one who had a surprising capacity for such objective feedback. He was very interested in improving his professional competence, partly because he was an ambitious man, and partly because he was a person who sincerely wanted to do the best he could for the children in his classes.

Over a period of several months I presented data to him, and I tried to guide him more or less gently to a broadened cultural perspective on himself, his students, and his teaching. At times, this being a mutual and cooperative relationship, he guided me, and in doing so contributed to my understanding of process in cultural transmission. We explored together his cultural background, his experience in the teacher-training institution, and the specific ways in which the dynamics resultant from this combination of cultural influences was expressed in his selective response to his students. Sometimes he was chagrined, sometimes depressed and self-doubting, sometimes angered, but always intensely interested and frequently very surprised. As a result, his perspective and understanding were broadened significantly, and he was able to interact more effectively with the broad cultural range represented by his students. He was able to do so because he had acquired a knowledge of his own cultural position, its influence upon him, the cultural range of his students, and his selective relationship within this range. I do not think he underwent a significant change in personality. It was not my intent, at least, to effect such a change. He did undergo a change in his cultural scope.

My use of the values-projective techniques in my education classes, and the analysis of data revealed by them in those classes, is an attempt to provide cultural therapy before the cultural patterns are activated in the classroom. I have no direct measure of their effectiveness. Students tell me, and give evidence in their behavior, of having experienced "cultural shock." They are able to place themselves in the matrix of values revealed in the analysis, and presumably are able to anticipate some of the ways in which their position may be a determinant in their exercise of the teacher's role, since this process is treated at length in class discussions, and documented with many illustrations.

In both procedures—the "feedback" process in cooperative case studies and in cultural analysis in the social foundations courses, the essential feature is that culture is treated as a third person. What I mean by this is simply that we are not dissecting the teacher, or the student's personality; we are dissecting his culture. His personal culture varies from the personal culture of others, but is directly reflective of the larger cultural context in which we all function. This makes a certain objectivity possible that is usually impossible when the issue becomes more personal and the individual's emotional defenses are more directly aroused. The subject of cultural therapy sees that his problem is not unique to him. It is shared in some degree with all of his colleagues—as a matter of fact, with everyone in his society. The "therapist" and the subject thus have the problem in common of understanding better how culture operates in and through of us.

I suggest cultural therapy as one direct measure we can take in our teacher-training programs to eventually reduce the self-defeating effect of much of our cultural transmission in American schools. I hesitate to suggest the case-study method as a direct measure because it takes a great deal of work to produce an effect on a single case. I am not optimistic about the probability that either approach will become widespread in the immediate future. We do not have the trained personnel to act as therapists. At this point I am not about to suggest that every teacher training institution start hiring anthropologists. Most anthropologists do not want to become therapists, even cultural therapists; they have other necessary and pressing work to do, and there are not enough to go around anyhow. I believe that with some help, the trainers of teachers can perform this function themselves, and the growing literature contributed by educators on the social and cultural process in American schools is an indication that this is already taking place.

Some Unresolved Dilemmas

Any highly schematic, but exploratory analysis of the kind I have presented should be concluded with some unresolved dilemmas. In reviewing the logic of this presentation. I am struck with the fact that in one sense I have had to attack an important source of some of the values I am trying to promote. I have argued for multiple channels of cultural transmission, and against single-channel transmission. I have also tried to show how conflicts in our culture are communicated to children, to the defeat of many of the professed aims of teachers. It has struck me with some force that until we understand the dynamics of cultural transmission more fully than we can hope to now, one of the insurances against single-channel transmission is conflict transmission. Of course, the pursuit of this point of view would eventually lead us to a position at dead center, where we acknowledge the defeat of our declared educational goals as desirable. But assuredly it is true that much of the healthy variation in personalities in our society, and certainly some of the innovations that are produced in our culture, issue from the conflicts patterned into it.

I think that the way out of this dilemma, if it is indeed a real one, is to acknowledge the conflicts in our culture more explicitly, even in the very act of transmitting them. And, perhaps, we may some day reach the point in our self-knowledge where we can at least be selective of the kinds of conflicts we transmit, and control better than we do the negative and unanticipated results of our transmission.

But there is another dilemma. Presuming that we somehow learn to control the results of our intended transmissions with increased knowledge of the relationship between the teacher and his culture, and between the teacher, his culture, the students and theirs, another order of question is raised—an ethical question.

The danger in knowledgeable and purposeful control is that this control could be used for purposes of inducing conformity, for purposes of transmitting values and patterns of behavior within a single channel. And with the trends toward conformity that seem well established in our culture, this seems to be a highly possible consequence.

We must, therefore, exercise extreme care that a growing awareness of the cultural dimension, and particularly of the values dimension and its transmission is not misused, by accident or intent. What I am arguing for here is that the teacher, as a cultural transmitter, achieve sufficient awareness of the multidimensional processes involved so that fewer potentially creative channels of communication, of transmission, be blocked, with the consequence that more children can be effectively caught up in the educative process. But the ethical problem I have raised is unresolved, and I believe that here we must turn to the philosophers for help.

THE INGLIS LECTURES

THE BURTON LECTURES

1957   George Dearborn Spindler. *The Transmission of American Culture.*

1958   Lawrence K. Frank. *The School as Agent for Cultural Renewal.*

THE INGLIS AND BURTON LECTURES

1960   Thomas Munro and Herbert Read. *The Creative Arts in American Education.*

1961   Joseph A. Schwab and Paul F. Brandwein. *The Teaching of Science.*

DEMCO 38-297